The Hundred T

THOMAS A. CLARK lives in the sm on the east coast of Scotland. He has published four previous collections of poetry, and numerous small books and cards with his own Moschatel Press. In the summer months, with the artist Laurie Clark, he runs Cairn, a project space for minimal and conceptual art (www.cairneditions.co.uk). Thomas A. Clark's work often appears as installations or interventions in galleries, public spaces or in the landscape. A large collection of such work has been installed throughout New Stobhill Hospital in Glasgow.

THOMAS A. CLARK

The Hundred Thousand Places

CARCANET

Acknowledgement

Thanks are due to the Scottish Arts Council for a writer's bursary during the making of this book.

First published in Great Britain in 2009 by
Carcanet Press Limited
Alliance House
Cross Street
Manchester M2 7AQ

A CIP catalogue record for this book is available from the British Library
ISBN 978 1 84777 005 9

The publisher acknowledges financial assistance from Arts Council England

Typeset by XL Publishing Services, Tiverton
Printed and bound in England by SRP Ltd, Exeter

The Hundred Thousand Places

once again
for the first time
morning

a sea mist closing
every distance
cliffs falling away
from the edge of a world
only half accomplished

listen
feel your way out
into what might
wave or rock
take form

you are not sure

there where you hover
over yourself
stay there

as if you were implicated
the lifting of the mist
from the water

the grey wake of a boat
unmoored at dawn

colour
the first
candour

the gorse flower
tenderness
nourished on rock
in a salt wind

primrose
of the islands
opened
by light
first primrose
of the islands

the lapwings
call to you
to confuse you

veering away
they call to you
to confuse you

a wide stretch of sand

you walk out
into space
as to
an appointment

with so much
space around you
intention
drops from you

here is where
forward momentum
runs out in
pure extension

no longer
ahead of yourself
in imagination
nor behind yourself
pushing on

you walk
above yourself
space spreading round you
the sand
bearing your weight

a path through the gold
of bird's foot trefoil
delayed by the pink
of thrift or campion

as it turns
in the long grasses
you are coloured
by events

there where
you lose yourself
brightness
takes your place

sit down on the rocks
impatience exhausted
thyme, thrift and clover
where the space is wide
hours should be wasted
thyme, thrift and clover

green islands
on blue seas
blue lochans
on green islands

drifting between
green islands
a red boat
on blue water

eight hundred
acres of heather
for the step
and the stride

on bright days
the world is brittle
the solid rock
is insubstantial

as you tread the deep
accumulations
a snipe cuts
a curve in space

between sea and sky
drifts of bugloss
a blue butterfly
lifting from the lyme grass

cormorant and herring gull
orpine and clover
sorrel and sea kale
redshank and plover

sunshine its climate
openness its aspect
detail its pleasure

the fields are drenched
in lark song
in detail
in dew

knee-deep in flowers
the red bull is lazy
muscle-bound
slightly drunk

as far as you can go
over the machair
there is only surface

it is a plane
of appearance
where nothing
is deferred

lacking depth
you walk on the richly
embroidered ground

the blue butterfly's
moment on the purple
thistle flower
is indolent

idly its hoarded
blue is unfolded
onto difference
then folded again

heard but not seen
the corncrake in the grasses
steps through fragrance

shy of exposure
seeking the shelter
of complexity and fragrance

asphodel, milkwort
eyebright, ling
the lovely particulars
brighter than their names

through crushed water-mint
through particulars you come
to a blue boat moored
beside purple vetch

if you stretch out
in the long grasses
your weight is distributed
over the headland
to rest as lightly
on the crushed grasses
as sky on sea

turning back from the sea
from margins and limits
behind yellow dune and grey dune
beyond the old hay meadows
follow your inclination
a drift of thistledown

the interior quiet
thistledown and bog cotton
a sweet scent
of cattle and wool

the place names
are exclamations
and sighs

not a stranger in the glen
without a rumour on the breeze
not a stray sheep on the hill
without word of it

along back roads
to far dwellings
single track
with pausing places
by vetch and clover

behind a straggle
of honeysuckle
the distances
laid on open
dog rose petals

through mud and manure
to hill farms
dark with neglect
a depth of fragrance
stored in the barn

at leisure a shape
lifts from rock and flaps
out over wastes
a few wing beats
taking it far

stretching inland
blackland and moorland
grassland and acid heath
a dark country
of heather and moor grass
of deer grass and moss

around the ruined
sheep folds and shielings
green islands
of sweet vernal grass
bent grass and fescue
rescue wilderness

a whim
of wind
in dry
whin thorns

a song
of wind
through bare
rib bones

whatever is lifted
by the wind is dropped
again into a calm
slightly ahead of itself

strong hill shapes
presiding over
pastoral slopes

sheep grazing
salmon in pools
of clear water

runnels of water
freshets of water
many voices

grey lichens
resting on branches
as if they had dropped

from the air

brighter than evergreen
fresh shoots on larch branches

their constancy is not
to continue in the same

but to return again
to spring, to morning
freshness and vigour

one song of water
picking up
from another

the slopes
constantly
spilling water

as you climb
it pours
around you

rushing, dashing
leaping to find
its level

stretch out
on the slope
beside water

where it leaps
headlong you resist
the inclination

there you go
but for a counter
weight or inertia

you do as you please
taking your ease
against the slope

the rock in the water
breaking the full
weight of the flow
produces melody

the rock by the water
broken by bracken
tormentil and heather
releases colour

from rock
heather
from astringency
colour

the many strands
of water are tied
in a woven braid
or plait of water
tossed in the early light

taking the slope
you glance back
at a grace or tress
of water and light

as you turn a corner
of the forest path
the face of the mountain
looms up before you

it knocks you back
for a moment
the force of it
straddling the path

you must gather
your wits and go
forward in a new
imposition of scale

as you climb the slope
mountain after mountain
appears on the horizon
flowers of altitude
they were waiting
there for you to come
among them
to look across at them
from your own height

what you feel
you can contain
what you see
you will become

the way is upward
through exhaustion
a scree of resistances

glittering muscovite
or white mica
little silver
sparks of sensation

along an arch
or anticline
the rocks lifted
and folded over
in inverse order

the lone violet
of altitude
finds shelter

scramble up
to the ridge
and look over

from complex
negotiations
to vistas
desolations

you are the first
thing the wind meets
as it whistles up
the side of the mountain

rocks, trees
mountains
solitary persons
swept up
in the wind

slopes of sunlight
slopes of snow
sit together
above the scree
innocent
of incident

on the mountain's shoulder
sit on a rocking boulder
rocking and hugging yourself

as you look out
over the hill shapes
you feel your way
over the hill shapes
your eyes walk
over the slopes

looking at hills
you are free of concern
filled with distances
volumes

where enquiry
hurries on
the hill shapes
take their time

take your time
the rise and the swell
of the hills are yours
their weight and implication
rest and aspiration

the hundred
thousand places
with a stone
and some grasses

the dwellings
in ruins
the stones
given back

all the little knots
of anxiety and tension
slowly unravelling
of affection and disaffection
slowly unravelling
the dried grasses trembling

if you move
lightly
events will start
up from your feet

crossing a moor
you are separate
pushed out from
the curve of the hill
or leaning against it

neither moor nor sky
including a sullen
sky and moor
you are broad
and resilient

butterwort
flower of the moor
purple flower
of emptiness

a basal rosette
of carnivorous leaves
the flower single
on a slender stalk

waiting
in emptiness

not the wisp of a breeze
in the lee of the day
among dapples and sedges
rushes and eddies
your pace slackens by
the loch of delay

a forlorn water
do not speak
your name here

a breath is enough
to fan the ripples
of water that run
deliciously in
around dwarf juniper

in the heat of noon
the cool of a pine wood
is refreshing
for man and deer

the songs of shade
are clear songs
thrilling through
gusts of cold

in the gloom the eye
flies to light
to light on a branch
and pause

among shadows
and half-lights
taking place
in their place
the deer
modest
and gratuitous

in a present
they do not
present to themselves
among trees
shedding
their predicates

let them
be there
in the shadows
let them be

who is it
in the pine wood
neither you
nor me

sheltered
the one who
sought shelter
dissolves

a stone from shade
carried for a mile
cool in the hand

there may be a hill
behind a hill
that will invite the gaze
to linger

grey-green behind grey
in looking you are there
it is all you require
this shape this colour

a steep-sided glen
you go on and on
deeper into green
led by implication

you are not where
you are but there
ahead of the given
in continual revelation

knee-deep in bracken
wade out into green
the displaced waves
of bracken fronds
settling around you

as you go forward
you are drawn
forward

green forms
rise up
in front of you

pouring into the visible
as if from some
invisible source

the colours glow
in and around you
you grasp or discard
relations and forms

what is at hand
supports or projects you
you have a mind to
green and gold

a common idiom
carries through
complex articulations
call it a place

it was not your
intention to bring
all your resources
here but you do

a hanging valley
of ash, wych elm, hazel
willow, birch, oak

dense cover of beech
light shade of ash

wintergreen, ramsons
sweet woodruff
guelder rose

hair moss, bracken
fork moss, oak fern
reindeer moss

under a tree
beside a stream
on top of a rock
habitats, dispositions

stands of pine
glades of bracken
ravines of filmy fern
thickets of bog myrtle

birch sapling curving
slightly twisting
out from the slope
rising and turning
in what might
be called a gesture
if a gesture can be
prolonged indefinitely

a breeze
of small birds
moving through
birch leaves

glen of the stones
moss growing over them
trees breaking through them
no path or direction
without plan or intention
you move among stones

to the left, a stone
a stone behind you
beside you a stone
about shoulder height
with moss-covered ledges
ridges and ravines

put your hand
on the hollow rock
place your hollow
hand on the rock

rocks fallen
from high places
keep their composure

you will have to go
all round it
to see it

have to stay
with it
to know it

far down
through green
a drone
of water

a green boat
by a hut
under alders
looking out

the path turns

don't follow it
wait to feel
the lure of it

turning you catch
sight of your own
shadow projected
on green

lured farther
deeper
you are immersed
in green

rising through
leaves and shadows
the imputed
form of the trunk

the attributes
held by
the attribution

the air is cooler
above the stream
that runs through mosses
under the pines

bright slope
of bracken
blue hollow
of bluebells

sit in a debris
of storm damage
thoughtless
in the sunlight

dusty little
butterfly
as if faded
by light

it has taken half a lifetime
to learn to sit in the sun
among primroses and violets
beside a dried adder skin
your back to a broken wall

the grey mare stands
with her back to the rain
tail and mane blown forward
a lean form in a field
facing towards mountains

coming down the hill
you are tall
take it easy
lean back
against the slope

the places
you have been
come with you
you bring experience
to evening air

cattle wade out
into the cool loch margins
among drifts of marsh marigolds
water-mint and speedwell
to stand and bellow
at the setting sun

you will need to know
who you are, to walk
by the solemn lochs

you will have to take on
the volume of a cloud
to move with circumspection

you will need to wear
boots of lead, to walk
by the solemn lochs

in a corner
of a field
unattended
a bonfire
consumes light

by the roadside
a wood
carpeted with wintergreen
wind in the high branches
stillness over moss

before you came here
was there dancing
and are the lugubrious
elders of the wood
pausing

the hill that was bright
is now dark
imperceptibly sensation
glows to emotion
then fades again

there is a faculty
that takes to the moor
and another that brings
you down to the shore

a part of you sheltered
by a gable wall
a part of you open
to the elements

a part of you substantial
and weathered as rock
a part of you mist
dusk and smoke

by an old mooring
a few steps
carved out of rock
go down to water

as if you might
step down into the sea
into another knowledge
wild and cold

far out in the dusk
where qualities mingle
a figure is standing
at the tide's edge